PYGMY GOATS

Everything You Need To Know About Pygmy Goats Housing, Health Care, Housing, Feeding And Nutrition, Habitat, Communication And Why They Make One Of The Best Breeds.

BY

RAPH FRANCIS

COPYRIGHT © 2024 ALL RIGHT RESERVED

TABLE OF CONTENTS

CHAPTER 1:
INTRODUCING PYGMY GOATS

CHAPTER 2:
COMPREHENDING THE BEHAVIOR OF PYGMY GOATS

CHAPTER 3:
SELECTING THE APPROPRIATE PYGMY GOAT

CHAPTER 4:
CONFIGURING THE ENVIRONMENT FOR PYGMY GOATS

CHAPTER 5:

NUTRITION AND FEEDING OF SMALL GOATS

CHAPTER 6:

PYGMY GOAT HOUSING AND SHELTER

CHAPTER 7:

PYGMY GOAT HEALTH AND DISEASE PREVENTION

CHAPTER 8:

PYGMY GOAT BREEDING AND REPRODUCTION

CHAPTER 9:

PYGMY GOAT HEALTH PROBLEMS AND HOW TO HANDLE THEM

CHAPTER 10:

PYGMY GOAT NUTRITION AND FEEDING

CHAPTER 11:

PYGMY GOAT HEALTH CARE AND COMMON ILLNESSES

CHAPTER 12:

PYGMY GOAT BREEDING AND REPRODUCTION

CHAPTER 13:

FREQUENTLY ASKED QUESTION AND ANSWERS (FAQS)

CHAPTER 1:

INTRODUCING PYGMY GOATS

One of the most well-liked varieties of little goats are pygmy goats, which are cherished for their diminutive stature, amiable nature, and versatility. Pygmy goats, descended from the West African dwarf goat, were originally introduced to the United States in the 1950s, mostly for use in zoos and scientific studies. But hobby farmers and pet owners soon came to love them for their endearing personality and small stature. Although their main purpose is frequently friendship and enjoyment, pygmy goats are maintained for a variety of purposes nowadays, from milk production to show animals to pets and companions.

What Is Unique About Pygmy Goats?

Because of their diminutive stature—they typically stand between 15 and 20 inches tall at the shoulders—pygmy goats are easily recognized. They are appropriate for both rural and urban settings because of their extreme adaptability to many habitats and their extreme hardiness, despite their small size. A range of coat colors, including caramel, black, white, and gray, go well with their little frame. Their pleasant looks and playful but attentive attitudes, along with their hues, make them a desirable option for goat lovers.

The sociable character of pygmy goats is one of the key draws for humans. They are very perceptive and inquisitive creatures who love connecting with people and other animals. Pygmy goats are gregarious animals that form close relationships with their owners. Because of their friendly dispositions and propensity to interact with people, they are sometimes referred to as "people goats". Pygmy goats are kind, patient, and generally non-aggressive, which makes them a great option for families, particularly those with kids.

In addition, compared to other livestock, pygmy goats need less maintenance. They can adapt well to a variety of living situations, don't need a lot of room, and aren't as prone to sickness as some bigger breeds. Although they do need adequate care and attention, novice goat keepers may easily handle them due to their manageable size and resilience.

Historical Context

Pygmy goats have their origins in Africa, where they were first crossed with dwarf West African goats. Because of their hardiness and capacity to survive in hostile environments, these goats were prized in their own country. Pygmy goats were brought to the United States in the 1950s as a result of imports to different zoos, where they were mostly kept for exhibition and scientific study.

Farmers and pet owners began to recognize the potential of pygmy goats as companion animals throughout time. They were a favorite among backyard farmers and hobby breeders because of their tiny stature and amiable disposition. Soon, pygmy goats were being raised for companionship and exhibition in addition to scientific purposes. The National Pygmy Goat Association (NPGA) was established in the United States in 1975, which helped to establish official standards for the breed and increase its appeal.

Nowadays, pygmy goats are seen as one of the greatest small livestock choices for those seeking a friend, amusement, and even some useful advantages, such small-scale milk production, from an animal that is simple to handle.

Pygmy Goats' Place in Contemporary Farming and Homesteading

Pygmy goats have a part in contemporary farming and homesteading activities, even though they are mostly maintained as pets or for recreational purposes. Although their milk production is very modest when compared to bigger dairy breeds, pygmy goats may serve as a supply of milk for small farms. However, because of its richness and high butterfat content, their milk is a fantastic choice for manufacturing handmade lotions, cheeses, and soaps.

Pygmy goats are great foragers on a farm. For the purpose of managing a garden or pasture, they may assist with weed management and plant control. They are excellent companions for other animals, such chickens or ducks, because of their inquisitive nature and grazing habits, which contribute to the upkeep of a varied and harmonious ecology on a small farm.

Pygmy goats are a wonderful addition to the homestead for anyone who is interested in sustainable living. Compared to bigger animals, they take less resources to keep, and since they are smaller, they require less room. Pygmy goats are adaptable to living in both rural and urban settings as long as they have the right care, food, and housing.

Pet Pygmy Goats

Pygmy goats are a popular pet choice because of their adaptability to household life. They make wonderful companions since they are very gregarious creatures who love interacting with people. The fact that pygmy goats may be lively, loving, and even naughty only serves to increase their allure as pets. In addition to their intellect, they may be taught to do basic tricks or duties like walking on a leash or responding to calls.

Nonetheless, it's crucial to remember that pygmy goats are livestock. It is normally advised to have at least two pygmy goats to keep each other company, since they are happiest when kept with other goats. If a solitary goat is left alone for an extended amount of time, it may get lonely and exhibit behavioral problems.

Although pygmy goats are also not too difficult to care for, they still need balanced food, appropriate housing, and routine veterinarian treatment to be healthy. They are an excellent option for those with little space because of their petite size, but they still need an area to play and wander. Pygmy goats are renowned for their climbing prowess and may readily escape if given the chance, so having a well-fenced yard or pasture is essential.

Final Thoughts

A flexible and enjoyable addition to any farm, ranch, or family are pygmy goats. Pygmy goats are a great combination of personality, practicality, and simplicity of care, making them a great choice for anybody searching for a pet, a milk supply, or just a loving companion. They have become one of the most well-liked breeds of miniature goats globally because of their fascinating history and appealing appearance in the present day.

We will explore the world of pygmy goats in more detail in this book, including topics such as selecting the ideal goat for your purposes and comprehending their behavior, health, and maintenance needs. Whether you're a seasoned farmer hoping to include pygmy goats into your operation or a first-time goat owner, this book will empower you with the information and resources you need to effectively grow and enjoy these fun animals.

CHAPTER 2:

COMPREHENDING THE BEHAVIOR OF PYGMY GOATS

Everyone interested in keeping these wonderful animals must comprehend pygmy goat behavior. Because of their distinct personalities, social behaviors, and communication styles, these animals are not only intriguing to watch but also gratifying to raise as pets or livestock. Having a thorough understanding of pygmy goat behavior is essential for building great relationships with them, ensuring their welfare, and simplifying management, whether you're keeping them as companions or for small-scale farming.

Pygmy Goats' Social Nature

Being gregarious creatures, pygmy goats flourish in settings where they may engage in interactions with both people and other animals. Because they are herd animals by nature, they need company in order to feel safe and comfortable. When left alone, a lone pygmy goat may experience loneliness, tension, or even depression. It is thus often advised to keep at least two pygmy goats together. This not only satisfies their social demands but also makes their living environment more peaceful and stress-free.

Pygmy goats create social structures among their herd whether housed in pairs or groups. Even if their social hierarchy isn't as strict or hostile as that of some other animals, it nevertheless has a big impact on how they interact with one another. While they could lead the way in obtaining food or cover, dominant goats often do it without acting too aggressively. But being aware of these social dynamics might help you spot instances in which a particular goat may need extra care or assistance—particularly if it is a frequently bullied or ostracized goat.

Their interactions with people reflect their social character. Due to their fun and loving nature, pygmy goats are wonderful companions for both people and families. Being inquisitive creatures, they often try to get their owners' attention by joyfully following you about or playfully standing on their hind legs. They can even be taught basic tricks, to come when called, and to react to names, which shows how intelligent and willing they are to interact.

Playful and Inquisitive Conduct

Playful and inquisitive, pygmy goats have some of the cutest characteristics. They are renowned for having an endless supply of energy and like exploring their environment. Pygmy goats are continuously looking for fun and excitement, whether it's by playing headbutts with their herd members, exploring new items, or scaling buildings. They will be happier and more content overall if you give them an opportunity to play and explore since this interest is part of their natural behavior.

Pygmy goats have a natural urge to be on higher ground and are skilled climbers. Their untamed forebears, who inhabited rocky environments, are the source of this trait. In addition to satisfying this natural want, giving them things to climb on, such as ramps, logs, or boulders, will keep them active both cognitively and physically. They often display their agility and balance by balancing on objects like hay bales, tree stumps, or even low fences.

But they're not only fun when it comes to climbing. In addition, pygmy goats like playing games with other animals and even people. They playfully headbutt one other, which is a normal habit for goats and not always an indication of hostility. But it's crucial to keep an eye on this behavior, particularly if they're interacting with young kids or smaller animals. Early play boundary education helps avoid any inadvertent injury or roughhousing with young goats.

Interaction and Voiceovers

Being talkative creatures, pygmy goats use a range of noises to interact with their human caregivers as well as with one another. Their main vocalization is a gentle bleating sound that they utilize to communicate a range of feelings and wants. They could bleat, for instance, if they're hungry, excited, or trying to get attention. With more time spent with your pygmy goats, you will learn to recognize their distinct vocalizations and differentiate between their many "goat conversations."

Apart from using their voices, pygmy goats may also convey messages via their body language. Their posture, tail, and ears are all used to convey their emotions. A goat with its ears forward and attentive is typically intrigued or interested in anything new, whereas one with its ears back may be feeling threatened or uneasy. Like with dogs, pygmy goats' waving tails are often indicators of happiness and joy.

You can more effectively attend to the needs and emotional states of your goats if you are aware of these non-verbal indicators. For example, a goat may be feeling ill or anxious if you see it lowering its head and avoiding eye contact. A self-assured goat, on the other hand, would walk with ease and hold its head high, signaling that it feels safe and well.

Territoriality and Aggression

Even while pygmy goats are often kind and non-aggressive, they may sometimes seem domineering or possessive, particularly when it comes to mating season or when there are male goats (bucks). Typically, this activity looks like headbutting, chasing, or posing around other goats. It's crucial to keep in mind that headbutting is normal goat behavior and isn't usually an indication of hostility. Goat kids often headbutt one other as a game or social skill exercise.

But, you may need to temporarily remove a goat if you see persistently violent behavior in it, such as excessive bullying of other goats or denying them access to food and water. Enrichment, wealth, and plenty of space may all reduce the likelihood of territorial disputes. Male goat neutering sometimes helps curb aggressive behaviors, especially in the breeding season.

It's also critical to understand that some pygmy goats, particularly those who feel threatened, may become defensive of their area or belongings. When bringing a new goat into an established herd, move slowly to give the current herd time to become used to the newcomer. This may facilitate the new goat's seamless integration by lowering any hostile or territorial behavior.

Creating a Bond with Your Mini Goat

It takes time, patience, and comprehension of your pygmy goat's behavior to develop a close relationship with them. Building a connection with them that is loving and trustworthy may be facilitated by playing with them, spending quality time with them, and giving them positive reinforcement. Many owners discover that their pygmy goats like hugging, petting, and even just sitting on their laps. Pygmy goats are clever creatures who react well to attention.

You may also use verbal praise or food or other positive reinforcement strategies to deepen your relationship. Because pygmy goats are food-motivated, you may teach them basic tasks, to come when called, and to follow you on a leash by rewarding them with treats during training sessions. Treats shouldn't be given to children in excess, however, since their diet should still be well-balanced and nutritious.

Final Thoughts

The many activities of pygmy goats reveal their gregarious, lively, and perceptive disposition, making them intriguing creatures.

Comprehending the communication, social hierarchy, and interaction requirements of your goats will enhance your experience as their owner and guarantee their welfare. Your pygmy goats' life will be enhanced and you will get closer by paying careful attention to their behavior and attending to their requirements.

CHAPTER 3:

SELECTING THE APPROPRIATE PYGMY GOAT

Choosing the appropriate pygmy goat is an essential step in guaranteeing that owning a goat will be enjoyable and fulfilling. Pygmy goats may be chosen for small-scale milk production, hobby farming, or even as pets. It's vital to take your time and choose the correct goat for your requirements and lifestyle. The important aspects to take into account while selecting pygmy goats are discussed in this chapter, and they include breeder reputation, age, gender, temperament, and health.

Determining Your Pygmy Goats' Objective

Prior to selecting a pygmy goat, you should decide what your main goal is for the animal. Pygmy goats may be used for a multitude of purposes, such as small-scale milk production or as cherished pets; knowing your objectives can help you focus your search.

- *Animals and Friends:* If you want to purchase pygmy goats primarily for companionship or as pets, temperament is important to consider. Seek for goats that are gregarious, sociable, and used to interacting with people. Regular handling from a young age increases the likelihood that a goat will be tame and at ease in the company of humans.

Production of Milk: Your attention should be directed to dogs, or female goats, if you're considering pygmy goats for small-scale milk production. Despite producing less milk than bigger dairy goats, pygmy goats' milk is rich in butterfat and may be used to make lotion, cheese, and soap. To guarantee excellent output, choose healthy females from a robust milking bloodline.

- ***Creation:*** A breeding program involving pygmy goats requires careful selection of does and bucks. Your attention should be directed at the goats' general health, genetic makeup, and ancestry. Pygmy goat breeders must pay attention to their genetic variety in order to prevent the health issues that arise from inbreeding.

Once your pygmy goats' purpose has been established, you may start examining each goat with a clear understanding of the qualities that are vital to you.

Comprehending the Temperament of Pygmy Goats

When selecting a pygmy goat, temperament is one of the most important things to take into account. Although pygmy goats are generally gregarious and sociable, each goat might have a unique personality. The ideal goats are those who are calm, inquisitive, and used to human handling. Shy or nervous goats might be more difficult to get along with, and if they haven't been well-handled, it could take some time to get them socialized.

Visit a breeder or merchant and see how the goats interact with people. Do they stay away from you or are they approaching you to look around? A goat that comes to you voluntarily or exhibits inquisitiveness without showing fear is probably well-socialized and would make a wonderful companion or pet.

Temperament is still crucial when selecting goats for breeding or milk production. During breeding, calm and laid-back dogs are simpler to milk and handle, while aggressive or very timid goats may be challenging to deal with. Spend some time getting to know the goats you are thinking about and seeing how they react to your touch. While shy or frightened goats may attempt to flee, amiable goats usually love being caressed. Remember that younger goats, or youngsters, are often easier to teach and socialize, which makes them a wonderful option for first-time owners.

Selecting the Correct Gender: Doe, Bucks, or Whitters

Making the option between bucks (males), does (females), or wethers (castrated males) is another crucial step in the selection of pygmy goats. The best option will rely on your objectives as a goat owner. Each gender has pros and downsides of its own.

Achieves: Does, or female pygmy goats, are an excellent option for anybody looking to produce milk, breed, or just have amiable companions.

Particularly when it comes to mating season, dois are often more laid-back than bucks. They are also simpler to handle in a domestic or agricultural setting and have a tendency to be more gregarious. A couple of doses might be a great option if your primary purpose for keeping goats is as pets.

- *Cash:* Usually, pygmy goat bucks—male goats—are utilized for reproduction. But because of their territorial and aggressive tendencies, bucks may be more challenging to handle, particularly in the mating season when they can become even more abrasive. During this period, bucks also emit a strong smell that may bother owners but is meant to entice females. Bucks are generally not advised for novices or for use as pets unless you want to produce pygmy goats. It's better to keep a buck apart from your does till it's mating season if you do need one for breeding.

- **_Context:_** For people who want pets but do not intend to reproduce, castrated male pygmy goats, often known as wethers, are a popular option. Compared to bucks, wethers are often more submissive and don't have the pungent smell of uncastrated males. They are just as trainable as they are, and they are loving and laid back. Wethers are often the greatest option if all you want from your goats are friends or for small-scale farming without breeding.

Remember that pygmy goats are herd animals and should never be kept alone when choosing their gender. For goats to be socially healthy, they need to have two or more, and the easiest way to do this is usually to have two of the same gender, either two does or two wethers.

Age and Health-Related Issues

The age of the pygmy goats should also be taken into account. Goats that are younger, or juveniles, are often simpler to socialize and train than adult goats. If given frequent attention from an early age, children may develop deep relationships with their owners and are more tolerant of unfamiliar surroundings. Since you may nurture them to fit your own requirements and preferences, beginning with young goats might be a smart alternative if you're new to goat raising.

But selecting mature goats has benefits as well, particularly if you want to breed or produce milk. Since adult goats have reached adulthood, you can get a better understanding of their personality, physical attributes, and state of health. It's also a good idea to choose a doe who has given birth if you're purchasing her for milk production, since this guarantees that she has milk production experience and ability.

You should always do a comprehensive health assessment on any goat you are contemplating, regardless of its age. Seek indications of a robust coat, clear eyes, and well-maintained physique. The goat's coat needs to be glossy and devoid of parasites, scabs, and bald spots. Look out for any respiratory symptoms that can point to an illness, such as coughing, wheezing, or nasal discharge.

Check the goat's hooves to make sure they are in excellent shape as well. Hooves that are fractured or overgrown may indicate inadequate maintenance. Inquire about the goat's medical history, including any shots or treatments it may have had, from the breeder or vendor. The medical history of the goat should be disclosed openly by the trustworthy breeder, who should also provide any relevant documents.

Choosing a Trustworthy Breeder

Selecting pygmy goats requires locating a reliable breeder. A competent breeder will put their animals' health and welfare first, giving them the right upbringing, diet, and socializing from an early age. They will also be happy to answer your inquiries and have in-depth knowledge about the breed.

Seek for breeders that belong to reputable organizations such as the National Pygmy Goat Association (NPGA). Best practices for breeding and care are often more likely to be followed by these breeders. Steer clear of big-time breeders or unskilled vendors who may not provide their goats the proper care.

Final Thoughts

Temperament, health, gender, and age are important considerations when selecting the ideal pygmy goat. You'll be in a better position to make an educated choice that guarantees a fulfilling experience as a pygmy goat owner if you take the time to evaluate your requirements and choose goats from a reliable breeder. Knowing the essential traits of pygmy goats can help you choose the ideal addition to your farm or residence, whether you're searching for milk producers, companions, or breeding stock.

44

CHAPTER 4:

CONFIGURING THE ENVIRONMENT FOR PYGMY GOATS

One of the most crucial things you can do to make sure your pygmy goats are happy and healthy is to provide them with a suitable habitat. Although pygmy goats are very adaptive creatures, they still have certain requirements for housing, area, fencing, and stimulation. You can guarantee their health and make care for them simpler and more pleasurable by providing a secure, cozy, and stimulating environment. The necessary components of creating a pygmy goat's ideal habitat—housing, space needs, fencing, bedding, and enrichment activities—will all be covered in this chapter.

Pygmy Goat Space Requirements

Despite their tiny stature, pygmy goats need plenty of room to roam, explore, and play. Goats need space to move about in order to exhibit their natural habits, in contrast to many other animals who are comfortable in small areas. Stress, boredom, and even health issues may result from a small space. It's crucial to provide them ample room to grow because of this.

It is generally advised to provide at least 200 square feet of outdoor area per goat. They have enough space to graze, play, and explore thanks to this. In case you want to maintain more than two pygmy goats, then kindly expand the room accordingly. Given their high levels of energy, pygmy goats will value having access to a bigger space where they may run, leap, and climb. Give them access to a variety of terrain, such as hills, rocky places, or grassy areas; this will keep them interested and enable them to imitate some of their natural behaviors.

Pygmy goats need both an outdoor area and an inside shelter where they may take cover from inclement weather, such as rain, snow, or intense heat. In order to keep them warm throughout the winter, the interior shelter has to have enough ventilation and insulation. Make sure the enclosure is large enough to accommodate the number of goats you want to keep, since each goat should have a separate place to rest inside the shelter.

Accommodation and Safety

Your pygmy goats' comfort and well-being depend on you giving them a strong, well-designed shelter. They should be able to sleep there, be shielded from the weather, and have a safe place to go at night.

Dimensions: The size of the shelter isn't important, but it should be roomy enough for every goat to be able to walk about freely and rest comfortably. For the interior housing, a minimum of 15 square feet per goat is advised. For instance, an enclosure of at least 30 square feet should be sufficient if you are keeping two pygmy goats. Larger enclosures, however, are usually preferable as they provide more room for comfort and mobility.

Substances: It is best to construct the shelter out of durable, weatherproof materials like metal or wood. Because pygmy goats may be hard on their surroundings, it's crucial to choose materials that can resist their inclinations toward climbing and rubbing up against objects. In order to provide adequate drainage, the roof should be slanted, and the shelter should be raised a little above the ground to avoid flooding during rainy seasons.

- *Airflow and Thermal Regulation:* Maintaining the shelter's freshness and avoiding the accumulation of ammonia from goat feces depend on adequate ventilation. Ensure that there are sufficient vents or windows to provide adequate ventilation. Insulation is required in colder locations to keep goats warm in the winter. Extra bedding will make them more comfortable during the winter months, and insulated walls or straw bales may assist keep heat.

- ***Access and Doors:*** The goats should be able to easily enter and depart the shelter via a large enough opening. They will be safe from possible predators if they have a door that can be locked at night. In addition, if you want to maintain a dairy for milk production, you may wish to include a separate section for feeding or milking in the design of the shelter.

Pygmy Goat Fencing

When building up a habitat for pygmy goats, fencing is one of the most crucial factors to take into account. Pygmy goats are not an exception to the rule that goats are legendary escape artists. The correct kind of fence may assist keep them from straying or getting into danger since they are nimble, inquisitive, and tenacious.

Height: Pygmy goats need a fence that is at least four feet high. Pygmy goats are skilled climbers and jumpers despite their tiny size. If you see your goats attempting to climb or leap over the fence, you may need to install taller fences. As an added measure, some owners choose to install a 5-foot-high fence.

- *Fence Type:* For pygmy goats, wire fences made of woven or welded wire work well. In order to prevent the goats from poking their heads through and becoming entangled, the distance between the wires should not be more than 4 inches. Steer clear of barbed wire since the goats might be hurt if they attempt to climb over it or escape. Make sure the electric fence is made especially for animals and that the voltage is suitable for goats if you want to use one.

- *Stability:* Pygmy goats may attempt to push or rub against the fence, therefore it has to be strong and securely fastened. Goats will quickly take advantage of any possible escape route, so be sure to frequently check for any holes or weak places. Goats are surprisingly good at opening unlatched gates, so make sure yours are firmly fastened.

Predator Defense: When planning your fence, you may need to take predator safety into account, depending on where you live. Your goats might be at danger from wolves, dogs, and other predators, particularly at night. To protect your goats from possible predators, you might add a predator-proof apron or reinforce the lowest portion of the fence.

Laundry and Bedding

Another crucial component of putting up a pygmy goat habitat is bedding. Your goats may relax in warmth, comfort, and a tidy environment thanks to the bedding. For goats, the most popular bedding materials are hay, wood shavings, and straw.

- *Inexact:* Because it is insulating and absorbent in the winter, straw is a common material for bedding. It is also simple to replace and reasonably priced. However, straw compacts easily and becomes filthy rapidly, so hygiene requires regular washing.

- **_Shavers of Wood:_** Another excellent choice for bedding is wood shavings, especially aspen or pine shavings. They provide the goats ample comfort, are simple to clean, and are absorbent. Cedar shavings should not be used because the oils in them might irritate the respiratory systems of goats.

Hay: Hay may be used as bedding even though it's mostly utilized for feeding. Hay could not be as absorbent as wood shavings or straw, and it is often more costly. If you use hay as bedding, be sure to clean it often to avoid moisture and waste accumulation.

Whichever kind of bedding you choose, it's critical to clean and change it often. Although they may pee and defecate in their resting area, goats are generally tidy creatures. Unclean bedding may cause an accumulation of ammonia and raise the possibility of infections or respiratory problems. At the very least, clean the sleeping area once a week. If necessary, particularly in the rainy season, clean it more regularly.

Mental Stimulation and Enrichment

Because they are bright and inquisitive creatures, pygmy goats need mental stimulation to keep them from becoming stressed or bored. Including enrichment structures and activities in their surroundings will assist maintain their interest and enhance their mental and physical health.

Climbing Frameworks: Pygmy goats appreciate exploring higher ground since they are naturally adept climbers. You may supply them climbing frames, such old tree trunks, big boulders, wooden platforms, and ramps. These structures encourage their natural activities in addition to offering physical activity.

- *Games:* Especially toys that they can push, tug, or fling about, goats love to play with them. Big balls, empty buckets, or even strong rope toys may keep kids occupied for hours. To keep things fresh and keep the goats from becoming tired of the same toys, rotate them often.

- *Platform for Grazing:* As grazers by nature, pygmy goats will be kept busy and fed a nutritious diet if you offer them access to a pasture or other green area. In the event that pasture is not available, you may promote foraging behavior by setting up a small grazing area with a variety of forage plants or by using a hay rack.

- *Socialization and Interaction:* Being gregarious creatures, pygmy goats like interacting with people and other animals. Every day, spend time with your goats—whether it's playing, grooming, or just watching them. This keeps them happy and well-socialized while also strengthening your relationship.

Final Thoughts

Pygmy goats must have a suitable habitat for their wellbeing, safety, and health. Every element of their surroundings, from offering enough room and a well-thought-out shelter to making sure they are securely fenced in and have access to enrichment activities, contributes to their general well-being. You can make goat ownership enjoyable and guarantee that your pygmy goats have healthy, happy lives by taking the effort to create a cozy and stimulating environment.

CHAPTER 5:

NUTRITION AND FEEDING OF SMALL GOATS

To maintain your pygmy goats' health, development, and well-being, proper food and nutrition are essential. A well-planned and balanced diet is essential to maintaining an animal's general health, immune system, and energy levels, just as it is for any other. Although pygmy goats are resilient creatures, their tiny stature and high energy levels need close attention to their nutritional requirements. The principles of feeding pygmy goats, such as the kinds of food they should eat, their nutritional needs, supplements, and feeding techniques to maintain good health, will all be covered in this chapter.

An Overview of the Pygmy Goat Diet

Like all other goats, pygmy goats have a sophisticated digestive system that is intended to break down fibrous plant matter. Their stomach is divided into four chambers, the biggest of which is the rumen, where microbes and bacteria aid in the breakdown of fibrous vegetation. Roughage must thus be the main food in their diet in order to maintain healthy digestion and general wellbeing.

Naturally, pygmy goats graze and forage. They would spend a large portion of the day searching for leaves, bushes, grass, and other plant material in the wild. Maintaining their health in a residential environment requires that they mimic this natural diet. Depending on their individual demands, their daily diet should consist of a combination of concentrates like grains or pelleted feed and roughage like hay or pasture.

Roughage: The Pygmy Goat's Dietary Basis

The bulk of a pygmy goat's diet should consist of roughage, since it is the most crucial element. The most popular forms of roughage are pasture and hay, which both have vital fiber that aids in digestion and maintains the healthiest possible rumen.

Hay: Your pygmy goats should primarily eat high-quality hay if you do not have access to pasture. High-quality hay aids in digestion with its diverse range of nutrients and fiber content. Alfalfa, timothy, or clover hay are the finest varieties for pygmy goats. Alfalfa hay is a great option for those that are pregnant or nursing because of its high calcium and protein content. However, timothy hay or a blend of grass hays is enough for adult goats' maintenance feeding needs. Hay that is moldy or dusty should be avoided since it may cause digestive or respiratory problems.

- *Forage and Pasture:* The best approach to provide for your pygmy goats' nutritional requirements is to let them graze on new grass, if you have the room. Since goats are naturally occurring browsers, they would rather eat weeds, bushes, and leaves than simply grass. It will be easier to make sure they get a range of nutrients if you provide a varied pasture with a combination of grasses, herbs, and shrubs. To avoid overgrazing and preserve the pasture's quality, rotate the grazing area on a regular basis. In addition to providing nourishment, access to pasture enables the goats to participate in their natural activities, which enhances their physical and emotional well-being.

Grains and Concentrates: Extra Feeding

Although the majority of your pygmy goat's diet should consist of roughage, you may supplement it with grains or pelleted feed. These are particularly crucial for goats with greater nutritional requirements, such developing young goats, who are pregnant or nursing, and breeding goats. However, grains should only be provided in moderation since overfeeding them might result in obesity and digestive problems.

Grains: Oats, barley, and maize are examples of grains that may be a rich source of nutrients and energy. They should only be taken in moderation, however, since consuming too much grain may cause potentially fatal digestive disorders including bloat and acidity. Giving an adult goat no more than one cup of grain per day is a general recommendation; however, the quantity should be customized to meet the requirements of each individual goat. The ideal uses for grains are as supplements or treats, not as the primary component of the diet.

- ***Chopped Meat:*** Pelletized commercial goat feeds are available, and they are specially designed to fulfill the dietary needs of goats.

They often include a well-balanced combination of proteins, grains, vitamins, and minerals. If you don't have access to a diversified pasture, pellet feed might be a practical method to make sure your goats are receiving all the nutrients they need. Because their nutritional demands vary, make sure you choose a feed created specifically for goats and stay away from diets intended for other animals.

Hydration and Water

Your pygmy goat needs access to clean, fresh water in its diet. Water must always be available for goats, particularly if they are consuming a lot of dry hay. Having access to clean water is crucial since dehydration may rapidly cause major health problems. Make sure they have access to water in both their indoor shelter and outside grazing space.

Make frequent checks to ensure the water hasn't frozen during cold weather. To keep water cold and entice goats to drink, place it in a shady spot during warm weather. Given their dietary preferences, goats may abstain from drinking if the water is old or unclean. To keep their water supply clean, they need to clean and refill their containers every day.

Dietary Supplements

The majority of a pygmy goat's nutritional demands may be satisfied by a balanced diet consisting of concentrates and roughage, although sometimes extra supplements may be required. Minerals are essential for strong bones and general health, especially calcium and phosphorus.

- *Loose minerals and mineral blocks:* Ensuring goats get critical vitamins and minerals may be achieved by offering them a loose mineral supplement or a free-choice mineral block designed particularly for them. The majority of livestock supply shops provide mineral supplements designed specifically for goats, and these supplements usually include vital elements like calcium, phosphorus, magnesium, and selenium. Ensure the mineral supplements are always accessible, and make sure the goats are utilizing them by checking on them on a regular basis.

- *Blocks of salt:* Goats also need salt, which is another necessary element. You may choose a mineral block that has salt in it, or a salt block can be given with the mineral block. This is particularly crucial if your goats are fed just on pasture since their fodder may not provide them with adequate salt.

Supplements for Vitamins: Extra vitamins could be required in certain circumstances, particularly for sick goats, dogs who are pregnant or nursing, and goats with particular medical issues. If a veterinarian advises it, vitamin supplements, such as those containing vitamins A, D, and E, may be given to their food.

Snacks and Healthful Foods

Treats may be a great way to strengthen your relationship with your pygmy goats and provide them enrichment, but they shouldn't make up a large percentage of their diet. For pygmy goats, some safe treats are as follows:

- Apples devoid of seeds
- Pumpkins - Carrots
- Bananas - Squash
- Melons - Pears
- Leafy greens, such as kale and spinach

A pet's digestive tract might be irritated by too many sweet or starchy treats, so always introduce new meals gradually. Furthermore, since poisonous plants like rhododendron, azalea, and oleander may be fatal, never feed pygmy goats these kinds of plants.

Feeding Procedures and Schedule

Small, numerous meals throughout the day are preferable than one big meal for pygmy goats. This feeding technique promotes a healthy digestive system and emulates their natural grazing activity. Your goats will graze all day if they are mostly on pasture, but if you are giving them hay or pellets, be sure you feed them many times a day.

In addition to feeding, be careful to often check the weight and physical health of your pygmy goats. If overfed, particularly with grains and concentrates, goats are prone to obesity. On the other side, malnutrition may result from inadequate feeding or consuming subpar food. To keep their body in a healthy state, modify their diet as necessary.

Final Thoughts

The secret to your pygmy goats' long-term health and wellbeing is to provide them a balanced diet. Your goats will stay happy, healthy, and active on a diet high in roughage, supplemented with concentrates, clean water, and important minerals. You can provide your pygmy goats with the finest care possible and enable them to flourish in their surroundings by learning about their nutritional requirements and creating a regular feeding schedule for them.

CHAPTER 6:

PYGMY GOAT HOUSING AND SHELTER

Being gregarious and energetic creatures, pygmy goats need secure, cozy, and well-ventilated housing in order to have happy, healthy lives. Ensuring that pygmy goats have appropriate shelter and surroundings is crucial for their safety from inclement weather, predators, and other possible dangers. The many facets of planning, constructing, and maintaining suitable housing for pygmy goats will be covered in this chapter, along with the space needs, flooring options, ventilation, temperature management, and other factors that are critical to their welfare.

Pygmy Goat Space Requirements

Choosing how much room pygmy goats need is one of the first things to take into account while building shelter for them. Despite being smaller than many other goat varieties, pygmy goats are nevertheless lively creatures who like playing and running about. They thus need enough room to move about and behave in their normal ways.

- *Space Inside:* There should be at least 15 to 20 square feet of indoor shelter area for each adult pygmy goat. This keeps people from being crammed in and gives them room to walk about comfortably. Enough room must be provided for every goat, since overcrowding may cause stress, aggressiveness, and the spread of illnesses.

- Garden Area: Pygmy goats need access to an outside space where they may graze, exercise, and explore in addition to inside shelter. It is suggested that each goat have at least 200 square feet of outdoor area, although larger spaces are usually preferable. Their physical and emotional well-being depends on having space to wander, play, and graze in a safe, fenced-in yard or pasture.

Shelter Features and Design

The design of the shelter for your pygmy goats should put the needs of the goats and the caregiver first, with comfort, security, and accessibility coming first. In addition to being predator-proof, it should provide protection from the weather, including wind, rain, snow, and intense heat.

- *Climate Safety:* Because goats are vulnerable to harsh weather, their shelter has to be built to keep them warm, dry, and wind- and wind-protected. It's crucial to create a roof that overhangs the walls in places where it rains a lot to keep water from collecting close to the shelter entrance. Insulating the shelter or adding more bedding can assist retain warmth throughout the winter months in colder areas. On the other side, to avoid overheating in hot areas, make sure there is plenty of airflow and shade.

- *Walls and Roof:* Your pygmy goats need protection from the sun, rain, and snow, which means they need a sturdy roof. Shingle or metal roofing is strong and offers high weather resistance. The walls need to be resilient to weather and strong. Common wooden buildings may be painted or treated to increase their longevity. Some prefer to build their shelters out of plastic or metal, but whatever material you decide on, make sure it will survive the weather where you live.

- *Windows and Doors:* Doors to the shelter should be simple to open and shut for your convenience and to keep intruders. Additionally, the doors should be big enough for you to readily enter and clean the shelter. Windows provide natural light and ventilation, but to keep goats from escaping or predators from entering, they should be covered with bars or mesh.

Carpeting and Pillows

The comfort and hygiene of your pygmy goats will be affected by the flooring you choose for their housing. Goats like to stand on dry, level ground, so steer clear of any flooring that becomes wet or slippery.

- *Gravel or Soil Surface:* A lot of goat shelters include a dirt or gravel floor with bedding made of wood shavings, hay, or straw. Goats may use dirt floors since they are simple to maintain and provide them a natural surface. But in rainy weather, they might grow muddy, so it's important to replace their bedding often.

- *Floor: Concrete:* Concrete flooring is favored by certain goat owners due to its durability and ease of cleaning. If the concrete isn't sufficiently covered with bedding, it might be harsh on the goats' legs and hooves. Make sure to apply a thick layer of straw or shavings to the concrete if you're using it for cushioning.

Material for Bedding: For bedding, pygmy goats often utilize hay, straw, or wood shavings. The goats' bedding keeps the shelter warm, keeps them comfortable when they lay down, and helps keep it dry. It's critical to regularly replace bedding to avoid moisture accumulation, which may result in the growth of germs, mildew, and parasites. Giving the goats more bedding during the cooler months helps shield them from the chilly floor.

Airflow and Ventilation

Keeping your pygmy goats in a healthy environment requires proper ventilation.

Respiratory problems, ammonia accumulation from pee, and the development of mold or mildew may all be caused by inadequate ventilation. Especially in the winter, make sure the shelter has windows or vents to let in fresh air while minimizing drafts.

- *Natural Air Exchange:* To encourage cross-ventilation, windows, doors, and roof vents should be positioned strategically. This keeps moisture and stale air from accumulating within the shelter. Airflow may be achieved via windows with screens or wire mesh, keeping out pests and predators.

- *Pneumatic Air Distribution:* Natural ventilation could not always be enough, particularly in bigger shelters or in regions with severe weather. Venting systems and exhaust fans may assist control airflow, maintain a clean, fresh atmosphere, and keep hazardous gasses out of the shelter.

Control of Temperature

Although they might be susceptible to very high or low temperatures, pygmy goats are generally resilient creatures. It's crucial to maintain the shelter warm enough in cold locations to avoid disease and frostbite. On the other hand, it's crucial to avoid heat exhaustion and dehydration in hot weather.

- *Cold Conditions:* The shelter should have enough insulation to retain heat during the cooler months. The shelter may be kept warm by using windbreaks, adding heavy bedding, and insulating the walls. In order to avoid freezing, some goat owners also utilize heated water buckets or lights. But exercise caution while using heat lamps since they might catch fire if not utilized correctly.

Sweltering Conditions: The shelter should provide plenty of shade and ventilation during hot weather. To avoid overheating, make sure you have access to fresh water and sections of shady outside space. Fans or misting systems may be added to the shelter if needed to help cool it down.

Predator Defense

Due to their tiny size, pygmy goats are susceptible to attacks by foxes, dogs, and coyotes. Their safety depends on making sure their outside space and shelter are protected from any hazards.

- *Delineation:* Sturdy fence at least four feet high should encompass the outside space. Given their agility and ability to leap, make sure the fence is high enough to keep goats in. The fence should also be sturdy enough to deter predators. Digging animals may be discouraged by using electric fences or by installing an additional layer of wire mesh at the bottom.

Security Doors: To keep predators out at night, the shelter's doors need to be securely locked. For extra security, goats should be taken inside the shelter at night.

Social Housing and Enrichment

Being gregarious creatures, pygmy goats flourish when surrounded by other goats. It is advised to keep two or more pygmy goats together to avoid boredom and loneliness. To keep them cognitively engaged, provide enrichment activities both within their shelter and outside.

Climbing Frameworks: Because goats like climbing and exploring, you may keep them occupied in their outside space by adding ramps, platforms, or wooden constructions. To avoid accidents, make sure these buildings are secure and robust.

- *Ambient Playthings:* Your goats may benefit from simple toys that provide mental activity, such old tires, logs, or hanging ropes. It's critical to engage in enrichment activities to avoid boredom, which may result in negative behaviors.

Final Thoughts

Ensuring the safety, comfort, and design of your pygmy goats' home is essential to their overall well-being. Your pygmy goats may live in a setting that is conducive to their success if you take into account factors like predator protection, ventilation, temperature management, shelter design, and necessary space. Not only would a well-kept shelter keep them safe from harm, but it will also promote their general wellbeing and enable them to have satisfying lives.

CHAPTER 7:

PYGMY GOAT HEALTH AND DISEASE PREVENTION

One of the most important parts of proper goat management is keeping your pygmy goats healthy. Despite their overall hardiness and disease resistance, pygmy goats may nonetheless develop a variety of health problems as a result of poor care, poor diet, or environmental conditions. Ensuring their long-term well-being requires a thorough health care regimen that includes immunizations, frequent check-ups, parasite management, and early illness diagnosis. The fundamentals of pygmy goat health care, such as typical health issues, illness prevention, and the best ways to maintain your goats' wellbeing, are covered in this chapter.

Regular Medical Attention and Supervision

Setting up a schedule for frequent health checks is the first step in keeping your pygmy goats healthy. Pygmy goats, like any other animal, benefit from regular monitoring to spot early symptoms of disease or pain. You may do these routine examinations during regular contacts with your goats or at designated intervals for health observation.

- *Physical State Rating (PSR):* Monitoring your pygmy goat's general health and nutritional state on a regular basis may be accomplished by taking a look at their body condition score (BCS). The BCS is a straightforward scale with 1 denoting an extremely thin animal and 5 denoting an obese one. A healthy pygmy goat should ideally have a BCS of 2.5 to 3.5. To find out whether someone is underweight or overweight, look at their ribs, spine, and hips. Then, modify their diet appropriately.

Alterations in Behavior: Goats in good health are gregarious, energetic, and vigilant. A change in behavior, such as tiredness, withdrawal from the group, hunger loss, or unusual vocalization, may be a sign of a medical problem. By identifying behavioral changes early on, you can address any issues before they worsen.

Coat, Ears, and Eyes: Check your pygmy goats' coat, ears, and eyes often for indications of parasite infestation. Good health is indicated by clean, clear eyes, a lustrous coat, and well-groomed ears. Ear mites, dull, rough coats, or discharge from the eyes may all be signs of untreated health issues.

Pygmy goat vaccinations

For pygmy goats, vaccination is an essential component of illness prevention. Your goats are protected from potentially fatal diseases by receiving regular immunizations. Among the essential shots given to pygmy goats are:

- *Tetanus and Clostridium Perfringens Types C and D:* This is the goat vaccination that is given out the most often. It offers defense against Clostridium perfringens-caused enterotoxemia (overeating sickness) in two forms and

Clostridium tetani-causes tetanus. In order to confer protection to the offspring, pregnant does get a booster shot a few weeks before to kidding. This vaccination is normally given once a year.

- *Reds:* Goats are not as susceptible to rabies as some other animals, but it is still a problem, particularly in locations where raccoons, skunks, and bats are among the fauna that may spread the illness. Depending on your region and the prevalence of rabies in the area, a rabies vaccine may be advised. To find out if your pygmy goats need rabies vaccines, speak with your veterinarian.

- *Lymphadenitis Caseous (CL):* Goats and sheep are susceptible to a bacterial illness called caseous lymphadenitis, which may lead to abscesses in the lymph nodes and internal organs. Although a vaccination for CL is available, it is not generally advised for all herds. See your veterinarian for advice on whether vaccination is necessary if you believe there is a risk of CL in your region or herd.

Control of Parasites

Pygmy goats are not an exception when it comes to the serious problem of parasites. Their health may be seriously impacted by both internal and external parasites, which can result in starvation, anemia, and, in extreme situations, even death. Maintaining your goats' health and parasite-free status requires regular parasite management procedures.

- *Internal Worm Parasites:* Pygmy goats often have internal parasites such as tapeworms, barber pole worms, and roundworms in their digestive tracts. Weight loss, diarrhea, anemia, and a deteriorated coat quality are signs of internal parasite infestation. A veterinarian's fecal examination may assist in identifying the exact kind of parasite and if your goat has an infestation of worms. Your veterinarian may provide a deworming program with the suitable anthelmintic (deworming drug) based on the findings.

It's crucial to rotate drugs as directed by your veterinarian and to deworm only when required since overusing dewormers might cause parasite resistance. Furthermore, grazing pastures should not be overgrazed, and other pasture management techniques may assist lower the chance of internal parasite infections.

- ***Alien Parasites (Mites, Fleas, and Mice):*** External parasites like lice, mites, and fleas may potentially harm pygmy goats. These parasites irritate the skin, induce hair loss, and cause itching. You may find external parasites early on in your goats' lives by giving them regular brushing and coat checks. Give your goat the necessary pesticides or parasite control items if you see that they are scratching a lot or getting bald spots. For external parasites, your veterinarian may provide safe and efficient therapies.

Typical Health Problems with Pygmy Goats

Even though pygmy goats are typically resilient creatures, they may be impacted by a number of common health conditions. Maintaining the health of your goats depends on your awareness of these problems and your ability to avoid or address them.

- *Deep:* Bloat is a potentially fatal illness that develops when a goat eats too much lush grass, grains, or some kinds of legumes, causing its rumen to swell with gas. An enlarged belly, pain, restlessness, and breathing difficulties are indicators of bloat. Limit access to rich fodder and steer clear of abrupt dietary changes to prevent bloat. Make quick contact with your veterinarian if you suspect bloat, since this disease has to be treated right away.

- *Hoof issues and foot rot:* Hoof problems in goats may include infections, foot rot, and enlarged hooves. It takes regular hoof trimming to keep your horses healthy and avoid issues. Maintaining dry and clean conditions in the shelter and pasture may help avoid foot rot, a bacterial ailment that flourishes in moist and unclean environments. Check your goat's feet for indications of infection and get veterinary advice if needed if it starts to limp or acts painful while walking.

- *Kidney stone urinary calculi:* Male pygmy goats are more likely to develop kidney stones, or urinary calculi, particularly if they are wethers, or castrated males. When minerals in the urine solidify and obstruct the urinary tract, this syndrome occurs. Limit the amount of grain that male goats eat, since this may raise the chance of stone development, and make sure they always have access to clean water to avoid urinary calculi. Because ammonium chloride makes urine more acidic, feeding them may also help avoid urinary calculi.

- *Conjunctivitis/Pink Eye:* An infectious infection of the eyes that results in redness, swelling, and discharge is called pink eye. Usually, germs, viruses, or irritants in the environment are to blame. Although pink eye seldom poses a serious risk to life, it may be uncomfortable and quickly spread among a herd. As part of the treatment, the afflicted goat must be kept apart, the eyes must be cleaned, and veterinary-prescribed antibiotic ointments must be used.

Disease Prevention and Biosecurity

Effective biosecurity measures are the first line of defense against illness in your pygmy goat herd. The term "biosecurity" describes precautions used to stop the entry and spread of illness inside a herd. Among the crucial biosecurity procedures are:

- *New Animals in Quarantine:* Always isolate new goats for at least two weeks before bringing them into your herd to make sure they don't have any parasites or infections. Before allowing the new goats to join the rest of the herd, get them evaluated by a veterinarian and keep an eye out for any indications of sickness throughout the quarantine period.

Sanitize and Decontaminate: Keep the goat's water containers, food locations, and shelter clean and hygienic on a regular basis. In addition to lowering the chance of parasite infestations, proper cleanliness helps stop the spread of infectious illnesses.

Limited Access for Visitors: Visitors should not be allowed to touch your goats, particularly if they have recently interacted with other animals. It is easy for diseases to travel from one farm to another by tainted footwear, clothes, or equipment.

Final Thoughts

Pygmy goat health requires a trifecta of regular care, prophylactics, and early diagnosis of any problems. You can guarantee that your pygmy goats enjoy long, healthy lives by giving them the right food, upholding strict biosecurity procedures, vaccinating them against parasites, and controlling parasites. Maintaining your goats' health and giving them the finest care possible requires regular health checks and veterinarian attention. Addressing any issues before they become severe is crucial.

CHAPTER 8:

PYGMY GOAT BREEDING AND REPRODUCTION

Pygmy goat breeding may be a fulfilling and instructive endeavor. Gaining a knowledge of the breeding and reproductive process is crucial, regardless of your goals: growing your herd, selling baby goats (kids), or just enjoying the experience of rearing young goats. Like all other animals, pygmy goats have certain mating cycles, gestation times, and need to ensure the health of the doe, or female goat, and her offspring. The fundamentals of pygmy goat breeding will be covered in this chapter, along with how to choose breeding stock, comprehend the heat cycle, manage breeding operations, and take care of dogs who are pregnant and their young.

Choosing Reproductive Stock

The quality of your breeding stock is the cornerstone of every good breeding operation. The effectiveness of the breeding process and the qualities inherited by the progeny will depend on the general health, genetic makeup, and general quality of the buck and doe, the male goats. Take into account the following aspects while choosing breeding stock:

- ***Well-being and Energy:*** The doe and buck should both have robust immune systems, be in excellent condition, and be devoid of any genetic flaws. Goats in good health have a higher chance of producing healthy kids. Before mating, make sure both animals have had their recommended doses of vaccines and deworming.

- *Details:* Conformation describes the goat's physical makeup and structure. Seek for goats with proportionate bodies, robust legs, and excellent body shape. This is particularly crucial if you want to raise goats for milk production or for exhibition. The doe's capacity to safely bear and birth her offspring is also impacted by confirmation.

Temperature: Both the doe and the buck should be of a composed and easygoing disposition. Although pygmy goats are typically amiable, some individuals may be more wary or aggressive. A breeding stock with a nice temperament will have a higher possibility of generating offspring who are also amiable.

Hereditary Background: Knowing the genetic heritage of both the buck and the doe can help you prevent inbreeding and lower the likelihood that inherited illnesses or deformities will be passed on. To make sure the animals are a good genetic match, if at all feasible, go into their pedigree and breeding history. Breeding animals with tight kinship ties may result in inbreeding depression, which can impair health and diminish the vitality of subsequent generations.

Gaining Knowledge of the Heat Cycle

Since pygmies are polyestrous, they have the ability to get pregnant many times a year. The time of the heat cycle when the doe is fertile and ready to mate is referred to as estrus. Comprehending the indicators and time of heat is essential for efficacious reproduction.

- *Duration of Cycle:* Pygmy goats go through a heat cycle that lasts between 18 to 21 days. The doe is responsive to the buck for 24 to 48 hours during each heat phase. The doe will go into heat again in around three weeks if she is not successfully bred at this time.

- *Warning Signs:* When a doe is in heat, there are several indicators. These consist of a vulva that is enlarged or inflamed, restlessness, increased vocalization, and "flagging" of the tail. In addition, the doe may indicate her interest in the buck by letting him to mount her or by remaining near him. When it's hot, some may have a small discharge from the vulva.

When to Start Breeding: The doe must be introduced to the buck at the appropriate point in her heat cycle. The best time to breed is during the first 12 to 24 hours after the doe starts to exhibit indications of heat. You may attempt again in her subsequent heat cycle if the doe is not successfully bred after one cycle.

Management of Breeding

It's time to oversee the breeding procedure once you have chosen your breeding stock and determined that the doe is in heat. A variety of techniques, such as artificial insemination and natural breeding, are used to produce pygmy goats.

Organic Breeding: The buck and doe are let to mate spontaneously in natural breeding. The most popular technique for producing pygmy goats is this one. Throughout the heat phase, the buck will often mount the doe many times. To avoid stress or overbreeding, the buck and doe might be split up after a successful mating.

Manual Reproduction: With hand breeding, which is a more regulated technique, the buck and doe are only permitted to be together during designated mating periods. This approach lowers the possibility of animal stress or harm while guaranteeing close monitoring of the breeding process.

- *Induced Pollution (IPL):* AI is a less popular way of breeding pygmy goats, but it may be used if you can get high-grade semen from a buck who has desired qualities. AI is often carried out by a veterinarian or other qualified specialist since it involves certain training and equipment.

Pregnancy and Gestational Health

The doe will begin the gestation phase, which lasts around 145 to 155 days (nearly five months), after a successful mating attempt. Pregnancy-related care is essential for the health of the doe and her offspring.

Diet: A well-balanced diet full of vital nutrients, such as protein, vitamins, and minerals, is necessary for pregnant women. A well-balanced grain diet, fresh water, and premium hay are essential supplies for pregnant goats. Refrain from overfeeding, since being overweight might pose challenges during childbirth.

- *Comfort and Shelter:* To help the pregnant woman feel less stressed, provide her a tidy and cozy place to live. Especially when her pregnancy draws to a close, make sure she has plenty of room to roam around and don't overcrowd her with other goats.

- *Vaccinations and Deworming:* If you think you may need any shots or deworming while pregnant, speak with your veterinarian. In order to protect the infants from infections, vaccinations such as the CD&T (Clostridium perfringens types C and D and tetanus) should be given a few weeks before kidding.

Postpartum Care and Joking

It is imperative that the doe get ready for the kidding (birthing) procedure as her due date draws near. The majority of pygmy goats give birth without any issues, but it's crucial to be ready and keep a watchful eye on everything.

Indications of Labor: A doe in labor may show symptoms including vocalization, pawing at the ground, restlessness, and frequent laying down. She may have a little vulva discharge, and her udder will become full and constricted.

- Process of Kidding: Usually, pygmy goats give birth to one to four children. Usually, giving delivery takes a few hours. Most do give birth on their own, but in the event of difficulties, including trouble delivering a child, it's crucial to seek veterinary care.

Care After Delivery: Once you've laughed, make sure the doe and her young are safe and secure. In order for the newborns to absorb colostrum—the nutrient-rich first milk that supplies vital antibodies—they should start feeding within the first few hours of life. Keep an eye out for any indications of postpartum difficulties in the doe, such as infection or retained placenta.

Final Thoughts

Pygmy goat breeding may be a rewarding endeavor, but it does involve careful preparation, monitoring, and administration. You may effectively grow your herd and take pleasure in the benefits of rearing healthy pygmy goat offspring by choosing high-quality breeding stock, comprehending the heat cycle, giving pregnant goats the attention they need, and implementing a secure kidding procedure.

CHAPTER 9:

PYGMY GOAT HEALTH PROBLEMS AND HOW TO HANDLE THEM

Pygmy goats are vulnerable to a range of health problems, just like any other animal. Keeping your goats healthy requires understanding common health issues and learning how to properly address them. This chapter covers the most common health issues that pygmy goats face, how to detect symptoms, and the best ways to prevent, treat, and manage your goat's general health.

1. Invertebrates

One of the most prevalent health issues with pygmy goats is parasites. These include internal parasites like worms as well as exterior parasites like lice and mites. If left untreated, parasite infestations may result in anemia, poor coat quality, weight loss, and even death.

- *Lice and mites, or external parasites:* Skin scabs, hair loss, and discomfort are all brought on by external parasites. Excessive rubbing, biting, or scratching at their skin may be seen in goats. Make sure your goats have a clean living space to avoid external parasites. Lice and mites may be removed with regular grooming, the use of the proper insecticidal treatments, and medicated shampoos.

- *Internal Worm Parasites:* For pygmy goats, internal parasites—especially gastrointestinal worms—are a major issue. An infestation of worms may cause diarrhea, weight loss, and a rough coat. Anemia from severe infestations has the potential to be fatal. A veterinarian can determine which worms are present by fecal tests. Frequent deworming is required, however in order to avoid resistance, dewormers must be rotated. Minimizing the danger of reinfection may be achieved by using excellent pasture management practices, such as alternating grazing areas.

2. Problems with the Hoof and Foot Rot

Goats who have bacterial infections in their hooves that cause foot rot experience discomfort, lameness, and trouble walking. Foot rot is more likely to occur in damp, muddy, or unclean living circumstances since these factors favor the growth of the bacteria. Overgrown hooves are another prevalent foot issue that may lead to pain and irregular walking.

Foot Rot Symptoms: Foot rot in goats may cause swelling, difficulties walking, and an unpleasant-smelling discharge between the hooves. In order to relieve pressure on the injured foot, they could sometimes lift their legs off the floor.

Avoidance and Management: Making sure that your goats have access to dry, clean living quarters is the greatest defense against foot rot. Maintaining hoof health and avoiding overgrowth requires regular hoof trimming. Treatment for foot rot usually consists of cutting the hoof to remove diseased tissue and using an antibiotic topical solution. Veterinarian-prescribed antibiotics may be necessary in severe situations.

3. Bloat

When gas cannot be expelled from the goat's rumen, the first stomach chamber, it may cause bloat, a potentially deadly illness. Goats who overeat or ingest large amounts of rich food, including grains or fresh beans, too rapidly may get bloated. It may also arise from abrupt nutritional changes, such switching from hay to verdant pastures without a time of progressive acclimatization.

Indications of Bloat: A bloated left side of the belly, pain, restlessness, fast breathing, and an unwillingness to eat are all indicators of bloat. In extreme circumstances, the goat can pass out or exhibit discomfort.

Avoidance and Management: Feed grain and rich meals sparingly and introduce new foods gradually to avoid bloat. To keep the goat's diet balanced and its rumen operating properly, give it plenty of hay. If bloat develops, quick intervention is required. Encouraging the goat to wander or massage its abdomen may aid in the evacuation of trapped gas. In extreme situations, you may have to contact a veterinarian for further care or use a stomach tube to release the pressure.

4. Immune System Problems

For pygmy goats, respiratory conditions like pneumonia are further prevalent health concerns. Usually brought on by bacterial or viral illnesses, goats with compromised immune systems or under stress are more susceptible to pneumonia. Respiratory issues may also be caused by environmental variables such as inadequate ventilation, crowded living quarters, and exposure to wet, chilly environments.

- ***Respiratory Issues Symptoms:*** A respiratory illness in goats may cause coughing, nasal discharge, dyspnea, lethargic behavior, and appetite loss. In extreme circumstances, the goat could have a fever.

Avoidance and Management: For goats to avoid respiratory problems, their living quarters must be clean and well-ventilated. Steer clear of unexpected exposure to cold or wet weather, and when circumstances are bad, give shelter. It's usually necessary to provide medications very away to a goat that has pneumonia or similar respiratory ailment. The right medicine may be prescribed by your veterinarian.

5. Overeating Disease: Enterotoxemia

Enterotoxemia, sometimes referred to as "overeating disease," is mostly caused by the naturally occurring bacteria Clostridium perfringens types C and D found in the goat's digestive tract. A goat may get really sick or even die from poisoning caused by germs that grow quickly when it eats too much high-energy food, such as grain.

- *Enterotoxemia symptoms:* Enterotoxemia in goats may cause abrupt onset diarrhea, bloating, stomach discomfort, and lethargic behavior. Goats may pass away unexpectedly in extreme circumstances without exhibiting any noticeable signs.

Avoidance and Management: Getting vaccinated against enterotoxemia is the greatest defense against it. For protection against clostridial infections, all pygmy goats should get the CDT vaccination. Additionally, make sure the goats' diet is well-balanced and refrain from overfeeding them grains or high-energy items. Goats with enterotoxemia need to be seen by a veterinarian right away since the illness may be lethal and worsens swiftly.

6. Toxemia During Pregnancy

Pregnants may develop pregnancy toxemia, mainly in the latter several weeks of pregnancy. When the doe's body is unable to keep up with the needs of developing babies, it results in an energy deficit. This often happens to those that are overweight or underweight when they get pregnant, as well as those who are carrying many children.

Pregnancy Toxemia Symptoms: Affected animals may have weakness, appetite loss, and gait difficulties. In extreme circumstances, the doe may enter a coma and, if untreated, perish.

Avoidance and Management: The key to avoiding pregnant toxemia is eating a healthy diet. A diet high in protein and energy is recommended for expectant mothers, particularly in the last weeks of pregnancy. A good grain mix and plenty of hay will assist make sure the doe has enough energy to sustain her growing young as well as herself. In the event that pregnant toxemia manifests, prompt veterinarian attention is necessary. The course of therapy may include administering energy supplements, fluids, and supportive care.

7. Pregnancy

Breastfeeding may develop mastitis, an infection of the mammary gland (udder). It may cause discomfort, swelling, and decreased milk supply. Usually, germs are the source of this condition. Mastitis sufferers may refuse to let their children suckle because it hurts so much.

- *Mastitis symptoms:* The udder could become warm, bloated, and uncomfortable to the touch. The milk may sometimes seem strange, clotting or having a yellowish hue. Additionally, the doe could show indications of pain and a decline in general health.

Avoidance and Management: It is essential to keep the udder clean, particularly during milking, in order to avoid mastitis. One way to lower the danger is to make sure the babies are well nursed and to clean the udder on a regular basis. Antibiotic therapy is required if mastitis develops. Anti-inflammatory drugs may also be suggested by your veterinarian to lessen discomfort and swelling.

Final Thoughts

Taking good care of your pygmy goats and acting quickly when problems do occur are essential to maintaining their health. The key to keeping a herd healthy is regular health checks, proper feed, a clean environment, and preventative measures like deworming and vaccinations. You can guarantee the long-term health and happiness of your pygmy goats by being aware of common health issues and understanding how to handle them.

CHAPTER 10:

PYGMY GOAT NUTRITION AND FEEDING

Pygmy goats need a balanced diet to be healthy, happy, and productive. Pygmy goats need a balanced diet to make sure they get all the vitamins, minerals, and nutrients they need because of their tiny stature and special nutritional requirements. Pygmy goats need to be fed with a diet that suits their nutritional needs at each stage of life, whether they are youngsters, bucks, who are pregnant, or nursing. It is not enough to just make sure they eat enough food. An extensive guide on feeding pygmy goats is given in this chapter, which covers the many kinds of feed, the right supplements, the amount of water needed, and how to control the diet to avoid frequent nutritional problems.

1. Knowing Pygmy Goats' Nutritional Requirements

Like other goats, pygmy goats have a four-chambered stomach that is intended to break down fibrous plant matter. This makes them ruminants. Roughage, such hay or fresh forage, should be their main food source; but, in some situations, their diet also has to be supplemented with grains, minerals, and vitamins. A balanced diet that prevents overfeeding or nutritional deficits while fostering healthy growth, digestion, and reproduction is the aim.

- *Protein:* A pygmy goat's diet must include protein, especially for young, developing youngsters, pregnant and nursing. Protein promotes general growth and the development of muscles. Alfalfa hay and other high-quality forages are great sources of protein.

- *Fiber:* Pygmy goats need their fair share of fiber for healthy digestion. Their digestive systems are built to break down fibrous plant material since they are ruminants. The main component of their diet should consist of hay as it is the most significant source of fiber.

- *Carbohydrate Energy:* Energy is necessary for pygmy goats to sustain their physiological processes, especially during development, pregnancy, and lactation. Oats, maize, and barley are examples of grains that are high in energy but should be eaten in moderation to prevent health issues like obesity and bloat.

- Size: Even though pygmy goats don't need a lot of fat in their diet, nursing does benefit from a modest quantity of fat. Vegetable oil and certain cereals are sources of fat, however they should only be consumed in moderation.

Minerals and Vitamins: Vital vitamins such as A, D, and E are crucial for immune system function, strong bones, and reproductive health. Elements such as calcium, phosphorus, and selenium are similarly vital, particularly for women who are expecting or nursing.

2. Pygmy Goat Feed Types

Creating an appropriate feeding schedule for pygmy goats requires an understanding of the many kinds of feed that are available. Similar to other goats, pygmy goats need a diverse diet in order to fulfill all of their nutritional demands.

- Forage and Hay: A pygmy goat's diet consists mostly of fresh pasture or premium hay. Hay gives them the necessary fiber to keep their rumen healthy and to help with digesting. Pygmy goats are often given two types of hay: legume hay (alfalfa) and grass hay (such as Timothy or Bermuda). Alfalfa hay is higher in calcium and protein, making it the best choice for developing youngsters, pregnant does, and nursing does. Grass hay has a lower protein content, making it an excellent alternative for

adult goats. For goats who have access to pasture, fresh fodder like grass, weeds, and bushes may also be a great addition to hay.

Grain: Goats' diets are often supplemented with grain, which is a great source of energy. Grain should be consumed in moderation, however, since overfeeding may result in health issues including acidity, bloat, and obesity. Pygmy goats are often fed grains including barley, maize, and oats. Grain is particularly helpful for developing children who need more energy, as well as expectant or nursing mothers.

Small Pellets: Specially prepared commercial goat pellets provide a well-rounded diet. These pellets are a practical and well-balanced choice for feeding pygmy goats since they often include a blend of grains, vitamins, and minerals. Pellets are especially helpful in situations where high-quality hay or fresh fodder are hard to come by. They must be fed with hay, however, as goats still need fiber for healthy digestion.

Additional Materials: Supplements may be required in rare circumstances, but for the most part, a pygmy goat's nutritional demands may be satisfied with a balanced diet of hay, grain, and fresh forage. Goat-specific mineral blocks or loose minerals need to be readily accessible at all times. These mineral supplements usually include salt, which is necessary for maintaining the right balance of electrolytes and fluids, along with important minerals including calcium, phosphorus, and selenium.

3. Aqueous Conditions

A pygmy goat's diet must include water since it is critical for digestion, nutrition absorption, and general health. Fresh, clean water is a must for pygmy goats at all times. The amount of water needed may change based on a number of variables, including size, age, and ambient conditions. Goats that are nursing, for instance, do need to drink more water in order to make milk, and they may also need to drink more water in order to keep hydrated. To stop the formation of germs and algae, make sure that water containers are cleaned on a regular basis.

4. Eating Throughout Various Life Stages

The dietary needs of pygmy goats change depending on their stage of life. For their general health, their diet must be modified based on factors like age, pregnancy, breastfeeding, or special medical requirements.

- Young Goats, the Kids: For growth and development, young pygmy goats need a diet high in protein and energy. Kids should be given premium hay after weaning, which usually happens at 8 to 12 weeks of age. They should also be fed a small quantity of grain or commercial feed that is specially designed for young goats. There should be access to fresh water and mineral supplements as well.

Adult Goats: Adult pygmy goats may be kept on a diet of high-quality pasture or hay with little to no grain supplements, including bucks and does who are not pregnant or nursing. Adult goats should never be overfed since excessive grain or rich food might cause obesity in them.

- ***Lactating and Expectant Mothers Do:*** It is true that pregnant women need more protein, energy, and calcium to sustain their growing unborn children. Because alfalfa hay is abundant in calcium and protein, it's a great choice for pregnant women. For added energy, it may also benefit from a modest quantity of grain during the last few weeks of pregnancy and throughout breastfeeding. Make sure to provide enough fresh water and a balanced meal to nursing mothers, since they specifically need extra water and nutrients to create milk.

- *Cash:* Although bucks typically need less energy than they do, they still require a well-balanced diet to be healthy. Bucks may need extra energy to maintain their weight and stamina throughout the breeding season. To assist fulfill their demands, give them some tiny amounts of food and high-quality hay.

5. Common Feeding Errors to Steer Clear of

Pygmy goat feeding involves cautious handling to prevent frequent errors that might result in health issues. Among the most typical feeding errors are the following:

- ***Grain Overfeeding:*** Feeding too much grain may result in major health problems including obesity, acidity, and bloat. Instead, grain should be consumed in moderation. Reduce your consumption of grains to prevent intestinal issues.

- ***Eating Hay of Poor Quality:*** Poor quality hay may cause respiratory difficulties, poor digestion, and other health concerns. It can also be dusty, moldy, or deficient in nutrients. Provide just the best, cleanest, freshest hay possible.

- ***A sudden change in diet:*** A goat's digestive tract might be upset by abruptly altering its food, which can result in problems like bloat or diarrhea. Make sure to introduce new food gradually to give your rumen time to acclimate, such as when switching from hay to fresh pasture.

- ***Ignoring Supplemental Minerals:*** Goats need certain minerals, particularly those like calcium, phosphorus, and selenium. Ensure that there is always access to mineral supplements in order to avoid deficiencies that may result in health concerns including weak bones, trouble with reproduction, or poor coat quality.

Final Thoughts

Maintaining the health, lifespan, and general well-being of pygmy goats requires feeding them a diet rich in nutrients and balanced in nutrients. You can guarantee your pygmy goats' long-term health and happiness by giving them premium hay, a reasonable quantity of grain, and the essential vitamins and minerals. Whether your goats are tiny babies, breeding does, or mature bucks, they will all stay in peak condition with proper nourishment suited to their individual life stages and access to clean water.

CHAPTER 11:

PYGMY GOAT HEALTH CARE AND COMMON ILLNESSES

Pygmy goat health involves proactive care, routine examinations, and knowledge of common ailments that may afflict them. Pygmy goats are susceptible to various health problems, just like any other animal, but many of them may be avoided with appropriate care, diet, and prompt veterinarian attention. This chapter will go over the essentials of caring for pygmy goats, including how to recognize symptoms of sickness and common ailments that affect these resilient, little goats. Whether you are farming pygmy goats or keeping them as pets, keeping them healthy is crucial to their long and fruitful lives.

1. Health Care Routines for Pygmy Goats

Providing your pygmy goats with routine preventive care is essential to keeping them healthy. These actions not only prolong life and improve overall wellness, but they help prevent illness.

- *Vaccinations:* Pygmy goats benefit from a simple immunization regimen, just like any other animal. The CD&T vaccine, which guards against tetanus, enterotoxemia (overeating sickness), and other clostridial infections, is one of the most often administered immunizations for goats. Every year vaccinations are advised for your goats, but always check with a veterinarian to be sure you're adhering to the right vaccine schedule for your area.

- *Deworming:* Internal parasites may affect goats, particularly in situations where they graze on pasture. Frequent deworming aids in worm load management, reducing anemia, malnourishment, and other parasite-related health issues. Tests for fecal egg counts may be used to determine the extent of infestation and direct deworming procedures. Deworming should only be done strategically when necessary since overusing dewormers might result in medication resistance.

- *Trimming the Hoof:* The constantly growing hooves of pygmy goats may become overgrown and uncomfortable, making walking difficult, and even prone to infections, if they are not regularly trimmed. Optimally, hoof trimming needs to be carried out every 4 to 8 weeks, contingent upon the topography and the goat's unique hoof development rate. Lameness and other problems like foot rot may be avoided by keeping hooves clean and well-trimmed.

Scoring Body Condition (BCS): An easy way to keep an eye on your goats' general health is to use a body condition score. You can determine if your goat is just right—not too skinny, overweight, or somewhere in between—by regularly examining their physical state. This is crucial in order to modify their diet and guarantee that they are getting enough nourishment without going overboard.

- ***Monthly Veterinary Examinations:*** Even though pygmy goats are often resilient animals, it's always a good idea to work with a veterinarian who specializes in goat care. Fecal testing, immunizations, and routine physical examinations may all aid in identifying any problems early on. Having a veterinarian on standby to handle unusual treatments or emergencies is also beneficial.

2. *Pygmy Goat Illness Signs*

The prognosis for a pygmy goat's health may be greatly impacted by early detection of sickness. Since goats are adept at concealing their pain, it's important to keep an eye out for any little behavioral or physical changes.

Variations in Taste: An abrupt change in appetite is one of the first indications that there could be a problem with a goat. Your goat may be experiencing digestive problems or a more severe ailment if it stops eating or drinking. Since goats are often voracious eaters, a lack of enthusiasm for eating may be cause for concern.

- *Apathy:* If a pygmy goat exhibits signs of illness, such as lethargy or lack of interest in its environment, it may not be feeling well. Lethargy has to be treated right away since it often indicates disease or discomfort.

- *Reduction of Weight or Unexpected Gain:* Unexpected fluctuations in weight may also be a sign of health issues. Rapid weight growth may be linked to metabolic disorders or an unhealthy diet, while weight decrease might indicate concerns such as parasites or nutritional inadequacies.

- *Constipation or diarrhea:* Goats in good health make tiny, hard pellets. Constipation or diarrhea (often referred to as scours) may be signs of an infection or digestive discomfort. In particular, diarrhea should be treated very ounce to avoid dehydration as it may indicate bacterial infections, food allergies, or parasites.

- *Anomalous Coughing or Breathing:* Pygmy goat respiratory issues may be brought on by parasites, bacterial or viral illnesses, or environmental variables such inadequate ventilation. Wheezing, nasal discharge, coughing, or hard breathing are symptoms that your goat could have a respiratory illness.

- ***Deviant Walking or Slumber:*** A goat may seem to be limping or have difficulties walking because of injuries, joint issues, or overgrown hooves. Lameness may sometimes also be a sign of internal health problems, such as diseases like hoof rot or mineral shortages.

3. Pygmy goat health issues and common diseases

Pygmy goats have an increased risk of several illnesses and ailments. Maintaining a healthy herd requires knowledge of these problems and how to avoid or cure them.

- ***Internal and external parasites:*** Worms and other internal parasites are often problematic for goats, particularly those that graze on pasture. If left untreated, parasites such as barber pole worms (Haemonchus) may lead to anemia, weakness, and weight loss. In addition, external parasites like lice and mites may cause pain, skin irritation, and hair loss. For parasite management, regular deworming and maintaining hygienic living conditions are crucial.

- ***Overeating Disease/Enterotoxemia:*** This is brought on by a bacteria called Clostridium perfringens, which grows in the digestive system and may spread quickly when a goat consumes too much rich food, especially grains. Toxin production follows, which has the potential to cause unexpected death. Both the CD&T vaccination and strict food control may aid in the prevention of this illness.

- ***Pneumonia:*** Tetanus may strike goats, particularly if they have wounds or other ailments. Bacteria that enter the body via wounds and punctures is what causes tetanus. The greatest defense against this potentially fatal illness is vaccination against the tetanus toxoid.

- ***Contagious Diseases:*** Goats are susceptible to pneumonia and other respiratory illnesses, particularly in poorly ventilated regions and in cold, wet surroundings. Coughing, nasal discharge, and difficult breathing are among the symptoms. The risk of respiratory infection may be decreased by keeping the goat's living space dry and making sure there is enough ventilation.

- ***Deep:*** Bloat is the result of trapped gas in the rumen, the first chamber of the stomach, which cannot be released. A common cause of this is overindulging in rich meals like grains or moist, verdant pasture. Bloat is a dangerous illness that has to be addressed right away since it may be lethal if ignored. Bloat is characterized by a bloated belly, restlessness, and breathing difficulties.

- *Encephalitis caused by Caprine Arthritis:* Goats that get the CAE virus may have arthritis, weight loss, and in rare instances, encephalitis, or inflammation of the brain, in their young animals. Children may be protected against CAE by being fed pasteurized milk or milk substitutes devoid of the parasite. CAE is mostly spread via contaminated milk.

- *Scald and Rotten Feet:* These are bacterial infections that cause discomfort and lameness in the hooves. Muddy and wet environments are often to blame for the development of these illnesses. Foot rot and foot scald may be avoided by regular hoof trimming, maintaining a clean and dry environment for the goats, and treating any early infection symptoms.

4. Health Issue Prevention and Management

When it comes to taking care of your pygmy goats' health, prevention is always preferable than treatment. You may significantly lower the risk of illness in your herd by putting sound husbandry practices into place, such as keeping living conditions clean, providing appropriate diet, and making sure frequent health checks are made.

Immune Fresh Goats: Diseases might enter your herd when you add new goats. Before introducing new goats to your existing goats, quarantine them for a minimum of two weeks and get them examined for parasites and other health concerns.

- *Offer Dry and Clean Housing:* Infections are less likely to occur in a clean, dry atmosphere, especially respiratory and hoof disorders. Maintain a clean bedding schedule and make sure the goat enclosure has enough ventilation.

- *Keep Track of Your Weight and Body:* Check your goats' physical condition on a regular basis to identify any possible health problems early. Unexpected weight loss or a thinning coat may be early signs of disease or malnutrition.

In summary, pygmy goat health care requires a proactive and conscientious approach. Your pygmy goats may have long, healthy, and fruitful lives if you take care of their health on a regular basis, provide them a good diet, and are aware of the main ailments that afflict them. The keys to managing and avoiding health concerns in your herd include keeping a solid rapport with a skilled veterinarian and being alert to early indicators of sickness.

CHAPTER 12:

PYGMY GOAT BREEDING AND REPRODUCTION

Pygmy goat breeding may be an exciting and fulfilling endeavor, but it also calls for preparation and appropriate information to guarantee the health and welfare of the dogs, or female goats, and the kids, or baby goats. This chapter will cover the essential elements of pygmy goat breeding and reproduction, from comprehending their reproductive cycles to making sure safe delivery procedures are followed. A deep grasp of the breeding process is necessary whether you are raising pygmy goats for your own pleasure, as part of a small farm, or to increase the size of your herd.

1. Comprehending the Reproductive Cycles of Pygmy Goats

Being seasonal breeders, pygmy goats' reproductive cycles are strongly correlated with the autumn and early winter seasons. With the intention of giving birth to children in the spring, when conditions are warmer and food is more plentiful, this natural breeding season takes place as the days become shorter.

- *Heat/Estrus Cycle:* The estrus cycle, sometimes known as "heat," in pygmy goats lasts for around 18 to 21 days. During each heat cycle, the doe will be open to breeding for around 24 to 36 hours. A doe's restlessness, vocalization, tail wagging, mounting behavior (against people or other goats), and swelling or redness of the vulva are all indicators that she is in heat. The doe will be more interested in the buck (male goat) at this time, and she could seem flirty by rubbing up against him.

Season of Breeding: Pygmy goats often start reproducing in late summer or early autumn and continue through the winter. Does not necessarily heat up throughout this season, particularly in areas with pronounced seasonal variations. However, pygmy goats may reproduce all year round in temperate or tropical climates.

- ***Maturity Age:*** Doeling may start between eight months and a year of age, or when they achieve sixty to seventy percent of their mature body weight. Their health may suffer if they breed too soon because they may not be emotionally mature enough to withstand the strain of pregnancy and childbirth. Conversely, bucks may become sexually mature as early as three or four months, so if you're not ready for breeding, you should keep young bucks apart.

2. Choosing Reproductive Stock

Choosing genetically sound and healthy breeding stock is essential to the success of any breeding operation. The buck and doe should be in excellent health, devoid of genetic flaws, and exemplary of the positive qualities you want to instill in your progeny.

Achieves: Look for adequate milk production, a fit physique, and strong maternal instincts in a doe before breeding her. When breeding, it is crucial that the doe is neither excessively thin nor too overweight since these traits might negatively impact fertility and the quality of the pregnancy. A doe who has reared her young well in the past is often a smart choice for future breeding.

- *Cash:* The genetic composition of the progeny is mostly determined by the buck, thus choosing a quality buck is essential. Seek for a buck that has solid conformation, a pleasant temperament, and has no past history of reproductive problems or genetic flaws. Selecting a buck with a track record of successful breeding is also crucial, if at all feasible.

3. *The Process of Mating*

A doe may be presented to the buck for mating after she reaches her heat. In order to guarantee successful pregnancy, the actual mating procedure is often rapid and occurs many times throughout the doe's heat cycle. The buck and doe should be split up after mating to avoid stress or overbreeding, particularly if the buck is belligerent or persistent.

Like many other tiny ruminants, pygmy goats breed rather well, and when all the right factors are in place, they have high conception rates. A doe will, however, come into heat again in around three weeks if she is unsuccessful in becoming pregnant during one heat cycle, giving her another opportunity to procreate.

4. Gestation and Pregnancy

Pygmy goats typically gestate for 150 days, or around five months, with a range of 145 to 155 days on average. The doe's body will alter in a number of ways as she gets ready to carry and give birth to her offspring.

Initial Pregnancy: Particularly in the early phases of the pregnancy, there may not be many obvious indicators throughout the first few months. Nonetheless, some may exhibit altered behavior, including being less energetic or more submissive. In order to maintain the health of the doe and her growing offspring, proper nourishment and care are essential throughout pregnancy.

- ***Integrative to End-of-Term:*** The doe's belly may begin to grow as the pregnancy goes on, and you can notice weight increase. Her udder will start to fill with milk in the last few weeks of pregnancy, ready for her to nurse the babies. During this period, it's critical to supplement the doe's diet with more high-quality grass, grains, and minerals to support her developing offspring as well as her own health.

Indications of Labor: The doe may begin to exhibit indications of labor as the due date draws near. These symptoms may include vulva swelling, a decrease in body temperature, restlessness, and nesting activity (such as digging or pawing at the ground). The ligaments around the doe's trailhead will also loosen in anticipation of giving birth.

5. Kidding Birth

For pygmy goats, the giving birth, or "kidding," procedure is usually easy and uncomplicated, particularly for seasoned moms. But, it's crucial to keep a watchful eye on the doe throughout childbirth in case help is required.

- *Work Stages:* Work is broken down into three phases. The doe will go through contractions in the first stage as the babies are ready to be born. This phase may last for many hours or throughout the whole day. The actual birth takes place in the second stage, when the children are delivered head first or breech (rear legs first). Though single or quadruplet births are also possible, the majority do give birth to twins or triplets. The placenta is expelled during the third stage, which usually occurs a few hours after the babies are delivered.

- ***Care After Birth:*** It's crucial to make sure the newborns start feeding within the first hour of their lives so they may get colostrum, which gives them vital nutrients and antibodies that are vital to their health. In addition to making sure the doe is in a clean, dry, and comfortable surroundings, keep an eye out for any indications of difficulties, such as a retained placenta or heavy bleeding.

6. Postpartum Care and Weaning

Depending on the youngsters' growth and the doe's milk supply, weaning usually takes place 8 to 12 weeks after birth. While minimizing stress on the doe, gradually lowering nursing time enables the offspring to make the switch to solid food. In order for the doe to recuperate from the stress of pregnancy and lactation, proper postpartum care includes making sure she receives enough nutrients.

To sum up, meticulous planning and management are necessary while breeding pygmy goats in order to protect the health and welfare of the dogs as well as the young. You may effectively raise healthy, happy pygmy goat children by being aware of their reproductive cycles, choosing good breeding stock, and giving them the attention they need throughout pregnancy and delivery.

CHAPTER 13:

FREQUENTLY ASKED QUESTION AND ANSWERS (FAQS)

Of course! For a book on raising pygmy goats, the following 12 frequently asked questions (FAQs) are included with their responses:

1. *Explanation of pygmy goats: Response:* A tiny breed of domestic goat, pygmy goats are renowned for their amiable disposition and diminutive stature. They are widely used for small-scale farming, as well as as pets and display animals. They are native to West Africa.

Even though they are little in height, they are resilient and adapt well to a variety of situations.

2. What are pygmy goats' essential needs?

Answer: For survival, pygmy goats need the following necessities:

- Shelter: To shield them from severe weather, provide a dry, clean, and draft-free shelter.
- Diet: Hay, pasture, grains, and fresh water in a balanced diet. They also need vitamins and minerals.
- Healthcare: Deworming, regular vaccines, and hoof trimming are necessary. Routine checkups aid in illness management and prevention.

3. How much room do pygmy goats require?

Response: Enough room is required for pygmy goats to wander and graze. Each goat should ideally have between 100 and 200 square feet, with extra room for a shelter. If housed in a pen or enclosure, make sure it's safe and has space for movement and socialization.

4. How can I tell whether a pygmy goat is ready for breeding? Response: A vulva that is enlarged and inflamed, restlessness, increased vocalization, and a readiness to mount or be mounted by other goats are all indicators that a pygmy goat is in heat. The doe may also display behaviors like waving her tail and approaching the buck to get his attention.

5. What is the pygmy goat's gestation period? Response: Pygmy goats typically take between 145 and 155 days to gestate, with an average of 150 days. This time frame may vary significantly based on the particular doe.

6. What should I do with a pygmy goat that is pregnant?

Answer: A pregnant pygmy goat should have access to healthy food, a hygienic and cozy birthing space, and routine health examinations. Keep an eye out for any indications of labor and make sure she has access to clean water and nutritious food. Learning about labor symptoms and possible childbirth issues may also be beneficial.

7. How should I respond to a sick pygmy goat?

Response: It's essential to see a veterinarian if a pygmy goat exhibits symptoms of disease, such as appetite loss, lethargy, diarrhea, or unusual behavior. Before the problem worsens, early action may help identify and cure it. Keep your surroundings tidy and adhere to a regular medical schedule to stave off disease.

8. When is the best time to deworm pygmy goats?

Response: Regular deworming is recommended for pygmy goats, usually every 6 to 8 weeks, depending on the parasite load and habitat. The right deworming regimen may be determined with the use of fecal testing. It's crucial to use dewormers sparingly and in accordance with veterinarian instructions since overuse may cause resistance.

9. What are the most prevalent health problems in pygmy goats? Response: Internal parasites, foot rot, respiratory infections, bloat, and dietary inadequacies are among the common health problems that pygmy goats face. Vaccinations, appropriate treatment, and routine health examinations may help avert these problems.

10. What should I do to be ready for the birth of pygmy goat children？ Response: In order to be ready for pygmy goat babies to be born, set up a dry, comfortable, and clean kidding place. Have basic birthing items available, such as clean towels and iodine for umbilical cord care, and keep a keen eye out for any indications of labor in the doe. Make sure the doe has food and water available, and be ready to help if things go wrong.

11. What is the diet of pygmy goats？ Response: Pygmy goats consume a wide range of meals, such as vegetables, cereals, fresh pasture, and premium hay. In order to guarantee a balanced diet, they may also need to take extra vitamins and minerals. They must always have access to fresh water. Taking into account their age, degree of exercise, and reproductive status, their diet should be modified.

12. Answer: Can pygmy goats coexist with other animals?

If the animals are introduced gradually and their interactions are watched, pygmy goats may live peacefully with other species, including sheep, other goats, and certain kinds of fowl. It's crucial to make sure that every animal has enough room, supplies, and is in good physical and mental condition. Keep an eye out for any indications of tension or hostility.

These frequently asked questions (FAQs) address important facets of owning pygmy goats and may assist new or potential owners in learning what to anticipate and providing good care for their animals.

Printed in Dunstable, United Kingdom